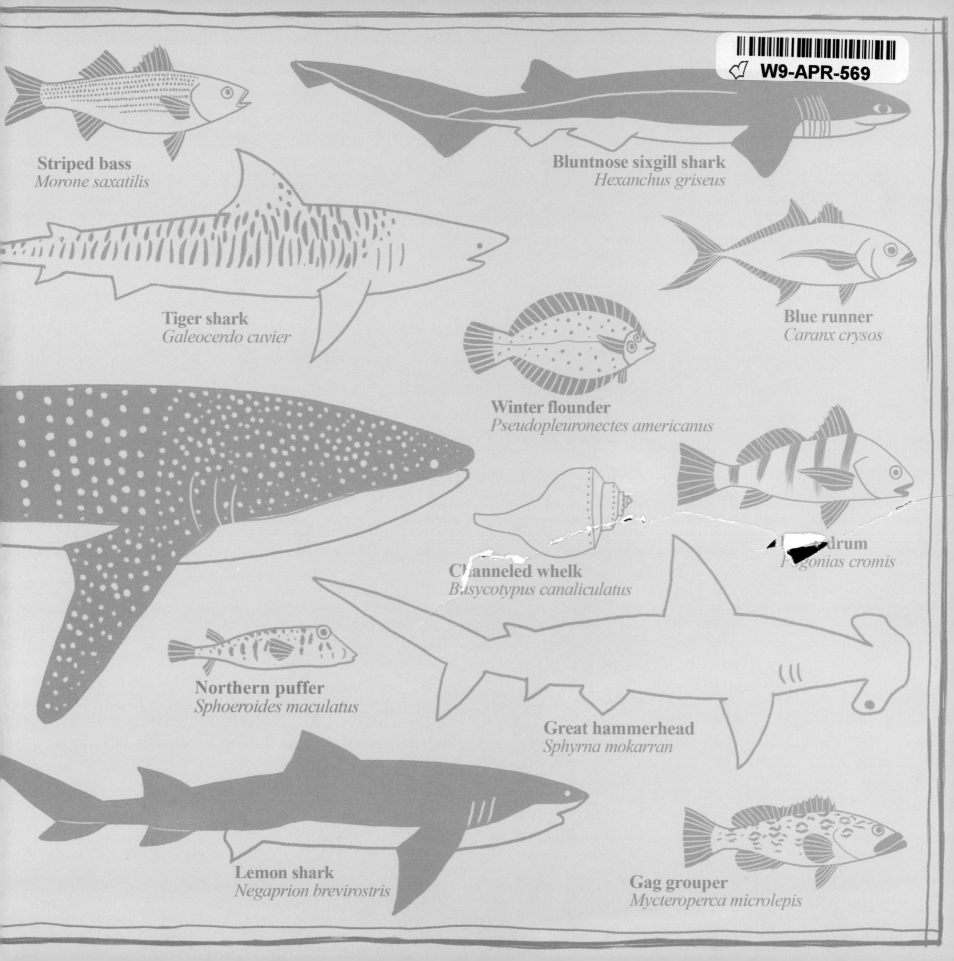

Striped bass
Morone saxatilis

Bluntnose sixgill shark
Hexanchus griseus

Tiger shark
Galeocerdo cuvier

Blue runner
Caranx crysos

Winter flounder
Pseudopleuronectes americanus

Channeled whelk
Busycotypus canaliculatus

Northern puffer
Sphoeroides maculatus

Great hammerhead
Sphyrna mokarran

Lemon shark
Negaprion brevirostris

Gag grouper
Mycteroperca microlepis

Merry Christmas 2020
Lucy

Enjoy your Book.
Love "Aunt Debbie"

SHARK LADY

The True Story of How Eugenie Clark Became the Ocean's Most Fearless Scientist

Written by Jess Keating • Illustrations by Marta Álvarez Miguéns

sourcebooks
jabberwocky

To my parents, for encouraging my big-as-a-whale-shark dreams,
and to Kathleen, for helping me reach them.
—JK

To my Baobab friends.
—MAM

It was Saturday, and Eugenie wanted to stay at the aquarium forever. She wanted to smell the damp, salty air and stare at the glittery rainbow of fish. She wanted to keep watching her favorite animals...

The sharks.

Eugenie pretended she was walking on the bottom of the sea. What would it be like to swim with her sharks? To breathe underwater with gills of her own?

More than anything, she wanted to find out.

When the summer came, Eugenie's mother took her
to swim at the beach in Atlantic City.

Stuffing sticky gum into her ears to keep the water out, Eugenie dove,
...down,
    ...down,
        ...down.

The salt stung her eyes, but she didn't want to miss a single fish. Constellations of sea stars speckled the pebbled sand. She imagined a silvery fin standing strong on her back, slicing through the ocean current.

To others, sharks were ugly and scary. But Eugenie knew they were beautiful. As she glided through the cool water, she wished everyone could see sharks through her eyes.

But the sharks were only in her mind, for now. Eugenie decided to learn everything she could about them.

So she dove...

...this time into books. Whale sharks. Nurse sharks. Tiger sharks. Lemon sharks. Eugenie wanted to know about them all. She also joined the Queens County Aquarium Society as its youngest member.

Eugenie's notebooks filled with sharks. They swam in her daydreams and on the margins of her pages.

At home, Eugenie's mother surprised her with an aquarium of her own.

A fifteen-gallon tank was much too small for sharks, but Eugenie saved her allowance to buy

guppies,

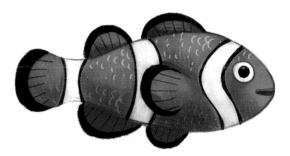

clown fish,

and coral-red snails.

It felt as big as an ocean in her room.
Their small apartment became an aquarium,
a laboratory, and a sanctuary.

As she grew older, many were still telling Eugenie what to do. Forget those sharks. Be a secretary! Be a housewife! Eugenie wanted to study zoology, but some of her professors thought women weren't smart enough to be scientists or brave enough to explore the oceans. And they said sharks were mindless monsters.

Eugenie knew better. Her dream was as big as a whale shark. So again, Eugenie dove.

She plunged into every course she could. Her laboratory became her home.
From sunrise to sunset, she studied how fish grow,

...how they behave,

...and how they were put together,
both inside and out.

Despite all of the people who didn't believe in her, Eugenie was becoming one of the smartest students in her field. Even after she earned her degree, many still doubted her.

But Eugenie's work was just beginning. Eager to make discoveries of her own, Eugenie finally dove into the open ocean.

In the Red Sea, Eugenie collected hundreds of fish, including three new species that had not been discovered before.

Red Sea sand diver:
Trichonotus nikii

Barred xenia pipefish:
Siokunichthys bentuviai

Volcano triplefin:
Helcogramma vulcana

On a research mission exploring the Palau Islands, Eugenie was diving alone when she encountered her first ever wild shark. She wasn't afraid. Instead, she thought it was beautiful.

In Isla Mujeres, she dispelled the myth that sharks must keep moving to stay alive when she swam through dark caves—still and silent—full of resting sharks.

Eugenie's daring heart grew bolder with each dive. Soon, they began to call her "Shark Lady." Eugenie had proven she was smart enough to be a scientist and brave enough to explore the oceans.

As her courage grew, she began to love and understand her beloved sharks more and more. But she never forgot many still believed that sharks were mindless killers. Because of their scary reputation, humans were hunting sharks all over the world. Eugenie knew that sharks weren't stupid or mean.

She was determined
to prove everyone
wrong.

Eugenie fished through her mind and devised a brilliant experiment.

Could she train a shark the way a person trains a dog?

Were sharks much smarter than anyone knew?

They were.

Eugenie was the first scientist in the world to train sharks and even learned they could remember their training for at least two months after.

Sharks were not mindless killers.

Sharks were beautiful. Sharks were smart.

They deserved to be studied,

...protected,

...and loved.

And Eugenie's dream
was now a dream come true.

SHARK BITES

Dangerous Monsters? No Way!

There are over 400 species of sharks, and of these, only about a dozen are known to be dangerous to humans, and encounters are extremely rare. The truth is, despite their fearsome reputations, humans are much more dangerous to sharks than they are to us. Every year, humans kill more than 100 million sharks. It's important to treat sharks with respect, but there is no need to fear them.

Sleep Tight?

Eugenie once swam in a cave full of peaceful, resting sharks suspended in the water. But were they really sleeping? Sharks breathe by using their gills to extract oxygen from water. Eugenie noticed that the caves with "sleeping sharks" had more oxygen than usual. She believed that this extra oxygen would make it easier for motionless sharks to breathe, so they didn't need to swim to pass water over their gills. Before confirming this discovery, most believed that sharks had to keep moving to stay alive.

No Toothbrush Here

Sharks have impressive teeth, arranged in rows along their gums. These teeth are constantly being grown and move forward in their mouths like a conveyor belt. Was Eugenie afraid of sharks because of their sharp teeth? No way! She was only bitten once in her life, and the encounter didn't happen under water! Once, on her way to a school visit with the mounted jaws of a tiger shark beside her in the car, Eugenie had to stop quickly at a red light. As she reached across the seat to stop the jaws from tumbling forward, the teeth chomped into her arm!

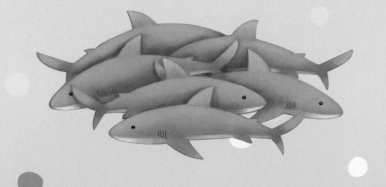

Sneaky Skin

Sharks can move extremely fast in the water and the secret to their speed is in their skin. Shark skin is made up of dermal denticles, which are more like teeth than fish scales. Some swimsuit designers have even created swimsuits that mimic shark skin to help Olympians swim faster in the water.

Big, Small, and Everything in Between

There is an incredible variety of sharks. The smallest in the world is the dwarf lanternshark at under seven inches long. The world's largest, the whale shark, measures over forty feet. Once, Eugenie was swimming with these giants in the Sea of Cortez. One swam very close to her—so close that she was able to grab hold of it! She let it carry her for a long time, until she finally let go when she realized she was far away from her boat.

Mermaid Purses

Some sharks give birth to live young. Others, like the dogfish, produce unique egg sacs that sustain their young. These leathery sacs are known as "mermaid's purses," and they provide the young shark embryo with a safe place to grow. Sometimes, it's possible to find a mermaid's purse on the shore if you look carefully!

Life at the Top

Sharks are apex predators. This means they're at the very top of the food chain in the ocean. Because of this, they play an important role in keeping food webs and prey populations in balance. Without sharks, ocean ecosystems would collapse.

Sharks are Old—Very Old

The first sharks appeared over 400 million years ago, and their descendants are still around today. They have survived five major extinction events, including one 65 million years ago that destroyed the dinosaurs!

EUGENIE CLARK TIME LINE

Eugenie earns her Bachelor of Arts in zoology from Hunter College.

Eugenie earns her master's degree in zoology.

1950

Eugenie becomes Dr. Eugenie Clark, earning her doctorate in zoology and a scholarship to study fish in the Red Sea.

May 4, 1922

Eugenie is born in New York. Her mother, Yumico, was of Japanese descent. Her American father, Charles Clark, passed away before Eugenie was two years old.

1931 — 1942 — 1946 — 1953

Eugenie publishes her first book, *Lady with a Spear*.

Eugenie discovers the belted sandfish (*Serranus subligarius*), a species of fish that can change its sex in as little as ten seconds.

Eugenie's groundbreaking work on lemon sharks is published. She is the first scientist to train sharks to push a target or ring a bell to receive food.

Eugenie visits the New York Aquarium at Battery Park and sees living sharks for the first time.

Eugenie's mother buys her a fifteen-gallon aquarium as an early Christmas present.

Eugenie becomes a professor of zoology at the University of Maryland.

Eugenie publishes a second book of her adventures called *The Lady and the Sharks*.

Eugenie begins writing columns and articles for *National Geographic* magazine.

Eugenie discovers the Moses sole (*Pardachirus marmoratus*) produces toxins that repel sharks.

Eugenie dives deep on her first trip in a submersible. In her life, she will make over 70 submersible dives to explore the ocean. These trips take her up to 12,000 feet deep!

1999

Eugenie moves to Sarasota with her family and begins working at the Mote Marine Laboratory.

1959 — 1968 – 1969 — 1972 • 1973 — 1986 — 2000s

Eugenie enters an underwater cave in the Yucatan Peninsula, full of resting sharks. She is the first to study them.

1981

Eugenie hitches a ride on the back of a whale shark.

1983

Egypt's first National Park, the Ras Mohamed National Park, is established, partly due to Eugenie's work in the area. She is a strong advocate for conservation and loves the beauty and diversity of the Red Sea.

2004

Eugenie injures her ankle on a diving expedition and is seen by doctors. They discover she has lung cancer, and she is treated with chemotherapy.

May 2014

Eugenie celebrates her 92nd birthday by scuba diving with a group of divers in Jordan and Israel.

February 25th, 2015

Eugenie Clark passes away in her home in the company of her family.

Author's Note

I wanted to tell Eugenie Clark's story for several reasons. As a scientist, Eugenie lived an incredible life full of hard work, passion, and undying curiosity. Through her legacy, she stood up for sharks, and in the process, stood up for herself. People assumed that sharks were evil and dumb. They also assumed that little girls shouldn't dream of swimming with them. On both accounts, she proved them wrong. Eugenie's life emphasizes how we must never let the world tell us what we can and can't do. It especially can't tell us how brave we will choose to be. I think this is a message important for young girls, boys—everyone—to hear.

And perhaps most importantly, as a member of the human race, I think Eugenie's belief in protecting the earth's species—no matter how different they are from us—is needed now more than ever.

There were many incredible tidbits about Eugenie's life that I wasn't able to include in the book. She was the first to develop "shark repellant," derived from flatfish to protect divers. She went on more than seventy submersible dives and even discovered a rare six-gilled shark, which she credits as her favorite species. She has written about her adventures in several books, and over 175 scientific journals and articles. She's been featured in over fifty television programs.

Nicknamed "the Shark Lady," Eugenie passed away at age ninety-two on February 25, 2015, but her legacy lives on. The Mote Marine Laboratory, for which Eugenie acted as Chair for Scientific Research, still exists. It's a place where young scientists can explore the oceans and discover Eugenie's sharks and just maybe find some of their own.

For more information about Eugenie and her work, you can visit mote.org online or read any of her numerous books. My personal favorite is *Lady with a Spear*, where she recounts an early experience diving under water: "This may read like science fiction, or a dream. It isn't fiction, but it is a dream—a dream come true."

I think she would be honored to inspire new dreams in young, curious minds today.

Bibliography

Clark, Eugenie. Lady with a Spear. New York: Harper & Brothers, 1951.

Clark, Eugenie. The Lady and the Sharks. New York: Harper & Row, 1969.

McGovern, Ann. Shark Lady: True Adventures of Eugenie Clark. New York: Scholastic Inc., 1978.

Eugene K. Balon. "The Life and Work of Eugenie Clark: Devoted to Diving and Science," Environmental Biology of Fishes, 41: (1994), 89-114.

Deborah Churchman, "It's Shark-Fin Rides—Not Soup—For This Ichthyologist," The Christian Science Monitor, 4 January 1982.

Juliet Eilperin, "The Rock Star Female Scientist Who Put Shark Research on the Map," The Washington Post, 27 February 2015.

Elaine Woo. "Eugenie Clark dies at 92; Respected Scientist Swam with Sharks," The Los Angeles Times, 28 February 2015.

Amy Huggins. "Eugenie Clark, Ph.D (1922-2015)" Archives of Maryland Biographical Series, Summer 2006.

Published by Sourcebooks Jabberwocky,
an imprint of Sourcebooks, Inc.
P.O. Box 4410, Naperville, Illinois 60567-4410
(630) 961-3900
Fax: (630) 961-2168
www.sourcebooks.com

Library of Congress Cataloging-in-Publication Data

Names: Keating, Jess. | Miguens, Marta Alvarez, illustrator.
Title: Shark lady : the daring tale of how Eugenie Clark dove into history /
Jess Keating ; [illustrated by] Marta Alvarez Miguens.
Description: Naperville, Illinois : Sourcebooks Jabberwocky, [2017] |
Audience: Age 4. | Audience: K to grade 3. | Includes bibliographical
references and index.
Identifiers: LCCN 2016030789 | (13 : alk. paper)
Subjects: LCSH: Clark, Eugenie--Juvenile literature. | Ichthyologists--United
States--Biography--Juvenile literature. | Sharks--Research--Juvenile
literature.
Classification: LCC QL31.C56 K43 2017 | DDC 597.3--dc23 LC record available at https://lccn.loc.gov/2016030789

Source of Production: Leo Paper, Heshan City, Guangdong Province, China
Date of Production: August 2019
Run Number: 5015776

Printed and bound in China.
LEO 10

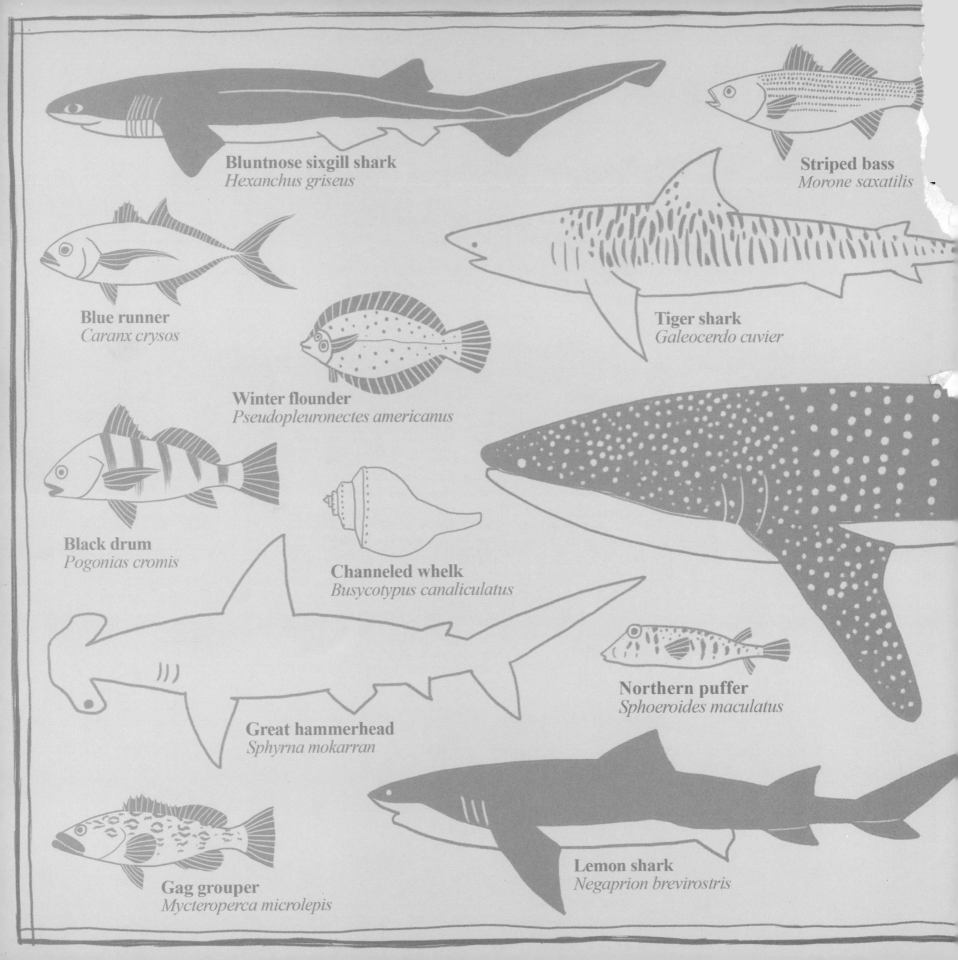

Bluntnose sixgill shark
Hexanchus griseus

Striped bass
Morone saxatilis

Blue runner
Caranx crysos

Tiger shark
Galeocerdo cuvier

Winter flounder
Pseudopleuronectes americanus

Black drum
Pogonias cromis

Channeled whelk
Busycotypus canaliculatus

Northern puffer
Sphoeroides maculatus

Great hammerhead
Sphyrna mokarran

Gag grouper
Mycteroperca microlepis

Lemon shark
Negaprion brevirostris